Masters of Music
THE WORLD'S GREATEST COMPOSERS

The Life and Times of

Stephen Foster

Mitchell Lane
PUBLISHERS

P.O. Box 196
Hockessin, Delaware 19707

Masters of Music
THE WORLD'S GREATEST COMPOSERS

Titles in the Series
The Life and Times of...

Visit us on the web: www.mitchelllane.com
Comments? email us: mitchelllane@mitchelllane.com

Masters of Music
THE WORLD'S GREATEST COMPOSERS

The Life and Times of
Stephen Foster

by Susan Zannos

Printing   1   2   3   4   5   6   7   8
        Library of Congress Cataloging-in-Publication Data
Zannos, Susan, 1934-
        The life and times of Stephen Foster/Susan Zannos.
            p. cm. — (Masters of music. The world's greatest composers)
        Summary: A biography of the nineteenth-century American musician whose many
        compositions include "Oh, Susannah," "Jeanie with the Light Brown Hair," "My Old
        Kentucky Home," and "Old Folks at Home."
        Includes bibliographical references (p.) and index.
            ISBN 1-58415-213-3 (lib bdg.)
            1. Foster, Stephen Collins, 1826-1864—Juvenile literature. 2. Composers—United States—
        Biography—Juvenile literature. [1. Foster, Stephen Collins, 1826-1864. 2. Composers.] I.
        Title. II. Series.
        ML3930.F6Z26 2003
        782.42164'092—dc21   2002022143

ABOUT THE AUTHOR: Susan Zannos has been a lifelong educator, having taught at all levels, from preschool to college, in Mexico, Greece, Italy, Russia, and Lithuania, as well as in the United States. She has published a mystery *Trust the Liar* (Walker and Co.) and *Human Types: Essence and the Enneagram* (Samuel Weiser). Her book, *Human Types*, was recently translated into Russian, and in 2003 Susan was invited to tour Russia and lecture about her book. Another book she wrote for young adults, *Careers in Education* (Mitchell Lane) was selected for the New York Public Library's "Books for the Teen Age 2003 List." She has written many books for children, including *Chester Carlson and the Development of Xerography* and *The Life and Times of Ludwig van Beethoven* (Mitchell Lane). Her great interest in composers inspired her to write this book. When not traveling, Susan lives in the Sierra Foothills of Northern California.

PHOTO CREDITS: Cover: AP Photos; pp. 6, 18, 31, 40 AP Photos; p. 9 Sandra Staas; pp. 12, 17, 20, 23, 25, 28, 36, 43 Corbis; p. 15 Center for American Music.

PUBLISHER'S NOTE: This story is based on the author's extensive research, which she believes to be accurate. Documentation of such research is contained on page 46.

The internet sites referenced herein were active as of the publication date. Due to the fleeting nature of some Web sites, we cannot guarantee they will all be active when you are reading this book.

Contents

The Life and Times of
Stephen Foster

by Susan Zannos

* For Your Information

This photograph of Stephen Foster is one of very few pictures that we have of him. He was always quiet and withdrawn. As a child he was neglected in a family that moved frequently and had no stable home life. As an adult he continued to be shy, never performing his own songs or appearing in public. While there are some romanticized portraits painted after he died, and statues commemorating his achievements, this is the only good likeness that remains.

Playing Hooky

F ive-year-old Stephen Foster went off willingly for his first day of school with his older brother, Morrison. Once there, however, he was given a strange book. The letters of the alphabet were presented in the form of Bible stories. It began, "In Adam's fall sinned we all." Stephen looked around in confusion. The other children were all reciting the verses.

In a book he wrote much later about Stephen, Morrison Foster remembered, "He (Stephen) was called up for his first lesson in the letters of the alphabet. He had not proceeded far in this mystery when his patience gave out, and with a yell like that of a Comanche Indian, he bounded bareheaded into the road, and never stopped running and yelling until he reached home, half a mile away."

As he grew older, Stephen would sometimes start out for school with his books and his lunchbox, but not get there. He headed for the riverfront instead. During the 1830's when Stephen was a boy living in the Pittsburgh area, rivers were the main routes of transportation. So he would end up sitting on a crate by a loading dock, watching and listening. Many riverboatmen were African Americans, either slaves or former slaves who had gained their freedom.

While they worked they sang their spirituals and work songs. Stephen was fascinated by the rhythms and the melodies.

Stephen was not a bad boy. It was just that school was not his favorite place. The only thing that really interested him was music. When he was just a toddler, his favorite activity had been playing his sister's guitar, which he called his "little piano." He would lay the instrument flat on the floor and pick out tunes.

When he got home in the evenings after a day of playing hooky down by the river, his mother Eliza's sad face made him feel bad. He didn't want her to worry about him. He knew she had enough to worry about with his father out of work and all of the children to feed and care for. Sometimes when the weather was hot in the summer, his mother would decide that instead of going to school, Stephen and Morrison could have their lessons with their sister Ann Eliza. And sometimes, when they didn't have a place where they could all live together, Stephen didn't have to study at all.

Some of Stephen's favorite times were when he was sent to stay with his old uncle, John Struthers, on his farm. The old man told his young nephew tales of his days as an Indian scout and spy during the Revolutionary War. Struthers seemed to be the only adult who thought that Stephen was talented, and predicted he would become a great man.

By 1840 when Stephen was 14, his parents decided to send him to his older half brother, William, to attend school. William was a successful engineer who did everything he could to help his family. Stephen began as a boarding student at the Athens Academy, but soon wrote to William, begging him to let him stay with him and go to a nearby school: "If you will let me board here...I will promise not to be seen out of doors between the hours of nine & twelve A.M. and one & four P.M. Which hours I will attribute to study,

The modern city of Pittsburgh is proud to claim Stephen Foster as a native son. The raw frontier town of Pittsburgh that Stephen grew up in was situated on the Ohio River near the coalmines and oil fields of Pennsylvania. It has since become a thriving metropolis of skyscrapers and commerce.

such as you please to put me into. I will also promise not to pay any attention to my music until after eight O'clock in the evening...the price is as cheap as I could live in Athens that lonesome place."

But Stephen didn't do too well with his promise to "not be seen out of doors." A classmate remembered that they often played hooky together, going for walks, wading in the streams, or gathering wild strawberries. The same friend said that Stephen's flute playing was beautiful and music was a passion with him. As much as Stephen wanted to please his practical older brother, he was unable to live without his music.

Shortly afterward, Stephen's father enrolled him in nearby Jefferson College and paid his tuition in advance. After a few days Stephen learned that another student was going into Pittsburgh and asked to ride along. He never went back.

His father was disgusted. William Foster could not understand why his son did not appreciate the opportunity for education. He wrote to William, "He does not appear to have any evil propensities to indulge; he seeks no associates; and his leisure hours are all devoted to musick, for which he possesses a strange talent."

Musical genius is a strange gift. No one can predict to whom it will be given, or when, or where. When it showed up in 19th Century Pittsburgh in this family devoted to business and commerce, Stephen Foster's peculiar talent was treated as a bad habit.

He was born into a world that valued the pioneer spirit. The men who were successful in that world built roads and canals and railroads, invented powerful machines, manufactured iron and steel. This quiet, dreamy boy who wandered off by himself and spent as little time as possible in school worried his family. They didn't know what to do about him.

There was talk of his joining the navy or attending the U.S. Military Academy at West Point. No one considered that it might be reasonable for Stephen to study the one thing he deeply loved, music. It was not considered an appropriate subject for a young man's interest.

But Stephen Foster became America's first great songwriter and today, nearly everyone knows his music. "Oh Susanna," "Way Down Upon the Swanee River," "Camptown Races," "My Old Kentucky Home," and dozens more have been American favorites for over 150 years.

River Boats

Before paved roads and railroads crisscrossed America, many transportation routes were along major rivers and canals. One of the most important routes went down the Ohio and Mississippi Rivers to New Orleans. Just about anything that could float was used.

Rafts were made by lashing together large logs. Then they would float slowly down to New Orleans. But it was impossible for them to go back upriver because they had no oars. So they were taken apart and sold for their lumber.

Flatboats were glorified rafts with flat bottoms and perpendicular sides. Many had large steering oars. But like rafts, they couldn't go back upriver. So they too were dismantled.

Keelboats were designed to return where they started. They were pointed at both ends and had a long keel, a central timber running from one end of the boat to the other. A deck protected the cargo below. They also had rudders and long oars for steering. A keelboat could make the long downriver trip from Pittsburgh to New Orleans in six weeks.

That was the easy part. Getting a keelboat back up the river was hard work. The boats could be rowed where the current was slow. In stronger currents the men poled the boat, setting the poles on the river bottom and pushing. Sometimes the men walked along the bank pulling the boat with towropes. Or two men could row ahead in a small boat, find a sturdy tree to wrap a rope around, and pull the keelboat up hand over hand.

Starting in 1811 with the *New Orleans*, steamboats became the most famous type of watercraft on the Mississippi. They could go upriver as well as down. Going upriver was slower, of course, but it did not require the hard labor that the keelboats did. They could carry much more cargo than keelboats or rafts. There was also a big demand for transportation of people. Steamboats could stop anywhere and pick up passengers.

But steamboats could be dangerous. They all had boiler tanks filled with water. Coal or wood fires heated the water to produce steam. The steam powered pistons that turned a big paddle wheel located at either the back or the sides of the boat. Under pressure to keep to their schedules, many steamboat captains would instruct their crews to stoke the fires to the maximum capacity. All too often the boilers exploded.

At their peak, hundreds of steamboats were on the Mississippi. Today, they have almost completely disappeared. But several still carry tourists who enjoy stepping back in time.

This flatboat being poled down the Ohio River is carrying livestock and cargo down to New Orleans. Flatboats were commonly used for transporting goods during the early 1800's. With their flat bottoms and squared sides, they were little more than rafts propelled by the current of the river. Unable to return upriver, the flatboats were broken up and sold for lumber in New Orleans.

An Invisible Boy

S tephen Collins Foster was born on July 4, 1826 at the family home in Lawrenceville, Pennsylvania, a few miles from Pittsburgh. It was the fiftieth anniversary of the signing of the Declaration of Independence, and his father, brothers, and sisters were at a picnic in honor of the event.

Stephen was the ninth child in the Foster family. His sister Charlotte was born in 1809, Ann Eliza in 1812. A brother, William Barclay, was born in 1814 but lived only 10 months. Shortly after the baby's death in 1815, an eight-year-old half-brother joined them and took the name of the dead child. That made the boy, who quickly became known as "Brother William," the oldest son. Henry was born in 1816, Henrietta in 1818, Dunning in 1821, and Morrison in 1821. One more boy, James, was born in 1829 but died the following year.

Before Stephen's birth, the Foster family seemed happy and successful. Their home, called the White Cottage, was built on 123 acres above the Allegheny River near Pittsburgh. It was more a mansion than a cottage, with cow barns, horse stable, hog pens, a smokehouse, and a summer kitchen. Stephen's mother, Eliza Foster, later wrote in her memoirs that their life then was like living in Eden.

Pittsburgh had been considered the western frontier when Stephen's father William moved there in 1796. It was a growing city, located near the extensive Pennsylvania coalfields. The coal was used in iron foundries and glass factories and helped the city to become prosperous.

William Foster found work with a merchant firm, taking goods down the Ohio River by flatboat to New Orleans. He returned by ship to New York and Philadelphia where he bought merchandise and brought it over the mountains to Pittsburgh. It was on one of these trips that William met Eliza Tomlinson, who was visiting relatives in Philadelphia. She came from a wealthy slave-owning family in Maryland. They were married in 1807 and became a part of Pittsburgh's best society.

William Foster owned a steam factory for a while, and later managed a stagecoach business. He was elected to the state House of Representatives. He purchased the land where he built the White Cottage and planned a housing development.

By the time Stephen was born, however, his father's business affairs were failing. One reason was that William Foster was an alcoholic. He defaulted on the mortgage on his property. Just before Stephen was born, the Bank of the United States foreclosed on the land, including the White Cottage. Soon afterward, the family had to move because someone had purchased the property. After that the family was constantly moving. Sometimes they lived with relatives, sometimes in boarding houses, sometimes in rentals. Stephen Foster wrote many songs about the longing for home, perhaps because he never really had one.

The White Cottage was the Foster family home when Stephen Foster was born on July 4, 1826. It was a spacious estate with cow barns, horse stables, hog pens, a smokehouse, and a summer kitchen. Stephen's mother, Eliza Foster, wrote in her memoirs that their life in the White Cottage was like living in Eden. The loss of this home was a tragedy from which the family never recovered.

"Stephen Foster was devastated by the loss of his home," wrote Ken Emerson, the author of *Doo-Dah! Stephen Foster and the Rise of American Popular Culture*. "His life was marked by tremendous instability after this, and he was always yearning for a home that he couldn't have. And that kind of nostalgia for a lost home is one of the deepest impulses behind Stephen Foster's music."

On top of the financial problems, there was tragedy. Charlotte, Stephen's oldest sister, died in October of 1829. Seven months later, baby James also died. Eliza Foster fell into a deep depression.

It was probably about 1832 or 1833 that, according to his brother Morrison, Stephen was in a music store and "accidently took up a flageolet (an early version of the flute) and in a few minutes so mastered its stops and sounds that he played Hail Columbia in perfect time and accent."

The boy's interest in music was considered a bad habit and a waste of time. It was fine for girls to take music lessons—singing and piano playing were admired skills for young ladies, and Charlotte had been an accomplished musician before her tragic death. But young men were expected to educate themselves for practical work in construction, businesses, and trades. The family hero, the man everyone looked up to, was Brother William.

As a young adult, he had joined a party of engineers and began a career that brought him recognition and wealth, helping to build canals, roads, and railroads. He eventually became chief engineer and later a vice president of the Pennsylvania Railroad. His continuing financial aid for his family helped them survive. Young Stephen admired and loved Brother William, but had no interest in his activities.

In 1833 William Foster Sr. took a temperance pledge and stopped drinking alcohol. This probably made things a little easier

for his family, although he spent as much time on temperance activities as he had spent drinking. Also, being sober didn't improve his business judgment. He wrote to Brother William thanking him for the $50 he sent for Ann Eliza's wedding and asking to borrow $200 more. He also asked his oldest son to find jobs for Henry and Dunning, saying, "I can't keep them together, they are both good boys."

After Ann Eliza was married, Stephen's mother took him and his sister Henrietta on a steamboat trip downriver to Cincinnati and on to Kentucky. They visited Eliza's relatives in Louisville. This was Stephen's only childhood visit to the state that would adopt one of his most famous songs, "My Old Kentucky Home," as its state song. He was seven years old.

Steamboats, like this one on the Ohio River by Louisville, Kentucky, became the most frequent method of transportation on America's rivers after 1811. Unlike the flatboats, they could go upriver as well as down, and they carried passengers in addition to cargo.

William Foster's affairs continued to go badly. He lost his job as a canal toll taker. He entered an election for sheriff but was badly defeated. He opened a general store in Pittsburgh with his oldest son's money, but the business failed almost immediately.

The family moved to a house in Allegheny that Brother William had bought. His mother wrote to Brother William in October of 1836, reporting that Stephen "had recovered from the whooping cough" and "was going to school with Morrison."

As usual, school did not receive Stephen's full attention. He much preferred playing his flute.

And he was already setting out on the path that would make him famous. ◆

The State of Kentucky was honored with this commemorative quarter in 2001. Stephen Foster's well-known ballad, "My Old Kentucky Home," is the official state song of Kentucky and is featured on the coin along with Federal Hill Mansion, the home of Foster's cousins whom he visited in Kentucky.

The Underground Railroad

The Underground Railroad wasn't underground. Nor was it an actual railroad. But it had plenty of "passengers." It was a secret route that about 100,000 African American slaves used to escape from their owners in the South for about 30 years before the Civil War started. Other slaves, free black citizens, and sympathetic white people helped them along the way.

Harriet Tubman

The first "tracks" were laid in 1831 when an editor in Boston, Massachusetts named William Lloyd Garrison began publishing a newspaper called *The Liberator.* He believed that slavery should be abolished. There were many other people in the northern states, where slavery was illegal, who felt the same way. They were soon called "abolitionists." Some of them operated "safe houses" where slaves could rest along their route to freedom. A lantern hung on a hitching post was the signal of a safe house.

William Lloyd Garrison

But in 1850 the United States Congress passed the Fugitive Slave Act. This law said that a slave could be caught anywhere in the U.S. and returned to his or her owner. Bounty hunters made money by finding slaves. So to be safe, the slaves had to make it to Canada. The Canadian government would not return escaped slaves to the U.S.

Some escaped slaves became "conductors" on the Underground Railroad. They would return to the South to help other slaves escape to freedom. This was very dangerous because they could be captured themselves and returned to slavery. One of the most successful conductors was Harriet Tubman. She grew up in slavery and escaped to the North, but she returned to help her family escape. After her family members were safe she went back for others. Tubman helped over 300 slaves find their way to freedom.

One of the Underground Railroad's main routes led through Wilmington, Delaware where a Quaker businessman named Thomas Garrett was the "stationmaster." The Quakers were a religious group who opposed slavery and operated many safe houses. After resting in Wilmington, the fugitives journeyed on to Philadelphia where William Still, a freeborn black merchant, helped them. Then they crossed the Appalachian Mountains to Rochester, New York, on the shore of Lake Erie. Frederick Douglass, himself an escaped slave, published an abolitionist newspaper there called the *North Star.* He helped the tired travelers find passage across the lake to Canada. Their journey, which had covered hundreds of miles over mountains and through swamps and forests, was over. They were free at last.

A blackface performer was a white man who covered his face with burnt cork to look like an African American. Groups of blackface musicians and dancers performed together in minstrel shows, which were the first truly American form of entertainment. The minstrel songs were sometimes learned from slaves on the plantations. Sometimes they were written by songwriters like Stephen Foster and later adapted by the slaves. And with some minstrel songs it was impossible to tell where they had begun.

Show Business

Although Stephen was usually a passive boy, Morrison described one period of activity that began about this time: "A thespian company was formed, composed of boys of neighbor families...The theatre was fitted up in a carriage house. All were stockholders except Stephen. He was regarded as a star performer, and was guaranteed a certain sum weekly. It was a very small sum, but it was sufficient to mark his superiority over the rest of the company."

Stephen performed comic songs written in the blackface dialect of popular minstrel shows, in which white men smeared burnt cork on their faces to impersonate African Americans. They sang songs like "Zip Coon," "Coal Black Rose" and "Jim Crow." Though these songs are obviously racist and insulting to African Americans, in a way they were like rock 'n roll when it began—a form of rebellion against older, more conservative musical forms. Stephen imitated these performers in his shows, which the boys performed three times a week. They made enough money so that they could go to the theater on Saturday nights.

Later, when Stephen was a reluctant 14-year-old student at Athens Academy, he composed his first known piece of music, "The

Tioga Waltz." It was written for four flutes with Stephen playing the lead part. After this he seldom performed in public and became upset if asked to play. Once when he and Morrison were invited to a party, the hostess asked him to bring his flute with him. He refused to go, but said that he would send his flute if she wished.

Stephen came under two quite different musical influences. One, representing European high culture, was represented by Henry Kleber, a talented musician from Germany. A church organist and choir director, he was a member of the Pittsburgh Philharmonic Society and also gave music lessons. Stephen Foster was one of his students. Probably Stephen learned something about classical music from Kleber. He certainly learned about popular romantic ballads. The first song Stephen published, in 1844 when he was 18 years old, was "Open Thy Lattice Love." It set a love poem to music.

The other musical influence came from Dan Rice, a circus performer. Rice became friends with Morrison and Stephen, probably because the boys showed up so often at his shows. He appeared in blackface as an "Ethiopian Serenader" singing crude songs in African American dialect.

Stephen also had a group of friends that he called "The Five Nice Young Men" in a poem he wrote about them in 1845. Each verse described one of the five. They shared an interest in music and would meet twice a week at the Fosters' home to sing harmony. Morrison Foster reported, "At that time negro melodies were very popular. After we had sung over and over again all the songs then in favor, Stephen proposed that he would try and make some for us himself."

The first song Stephen wrote for the Nice Young Men was "Lou'siana Belle." It was the first of his blackface songs to be published and the first that showed the influence of Dan Rice and the

Minstrel troupes of blackface performers grew larger as they grew more popular. Many of the most famous entertainers in America during the first years of the 20th Century got their start in minstrel shows. Al Jolson, called The World's Greatest Entertainer, is pictured second from left in this photo taken around 1900. Jolson went on to star in the first "talkie" (a motion picture with sound), The Jazz Singer.

coarseness of the minstrel shows. Stephen's next song, "Uncle Ned," was more sentimental. He was beginning to combine the black dialect of the minstrel songs with the romantic notions of the parlor ballads. It was a combination that was to produce some of the most popular music in America.

By the end of 1846, it was clear that the 20-year-old Stephen needed to go to work. The family could not afford to support him. His older brother Dunning had a partnership in a commission business in Cincinnati, getting cargoes for steamboats on the Ohio River. His company needed a bookkeeper. So Stephen traveled nearly 500 miles downriver from Pittsburgh.

The company was located right on the riverfront. When Stephen looked up from his bookkeeping ledgers and out the front window, he could see the steamboats lined up at the docks. Across the river was Kentucky with its slave markets. Runaway slaves crossed the river there on one of the routes of the Underground Railroad, their trip to freedom.

As a result, Cincinnati was one of the most racially mixed cities in the country. Stephen Foster had the opportunity to hear genuine black music while he was there. African Americans worked on steamboats as stevedores or stoking the boilers in the engine rooms. Along with the cargo and the passengers, they carried their music to the river towns.

Meanwhile back in Pittsburgh a new place of entertainment was opening, the Eagle Ice Cream Saloon. In August, 1847, the owner advertised "Musical Entertainment Extraordinary" and a dish of ice cream for a quarter. There was a different musical program every evening. The place did well, and before long the owner advertised a contest for the best "original words of an Ethiopian Melody." The winner would be determined by the spontaneous applause of the audience and would win a silver cup.

Riverside towns on the Ohio River, such as this one pictured in 1975, began because waterways were the main transportation routes when the country was young. Not only livestock and merchandise, but music and culture as well traveled up and down the rivers. Stephen Foster got the inspiration for his music from the African Americans working on riverboats.

Stephen's brother Morrison, who was still in Pittsburgh, sent him news of the contest. Stephen sent Morrison a copy of a new song, "Away Down South," to submit in the contest. The song didn't win, but it got the audience's attention.

The following month, Stephen sent another song. Like "Away Down South," this one got the attention of the audience in the Eagle Ice Cream Saloon.

Soon it would get the attention of the entire nation.

MINSTREL SHOWS

Before 1840, most of the musical culture of America arrived from Europe. Opera and classical music provided high culture. Circuses and comic theater kept the lower classes entertained. Not until the development of the minstrel show did Americans produce an art form of their own.

Most traveling circuses had a blackface singer as one of the acts. A blackface performer was a white man who covered his face with burnt cork to look like an African American. One such entertainer, Dan Emmett, was sitting around with three friends in his hotel in New York's Bowery during the winter of 1842. One friend was a dancer who played the bones, sawed-off lengths of horse ribs. Another played the banjo, an instrument that was origi- nally a gourd with four strings stretched across it brought from Africa by slaves. The third was a tambourine player and dancer. They were having a jam session and enjoying the noise they were making. They were also creating the instrumental line-up of the minstrel band.

Emmett and his friends called themselves the Virginia Minstrels. Instead of isolated acts in blackface, they presented an entire evening's entertainment. None of the elements of the show were original, but putting them all together was.

The show began with the four minstrels playing together. The bones and tambourine players were the "end men." They stood at either end and added comic relief with their jokes. In the second section, each entertainer presented a solo act. The final section of the show was a short play or a recreation of a plantation scene. The evening ended with a walk-around, or cakewalk, a kind of strutting dance.

The Virginia Minstrels stayed together for less than a year, but by the time the band broke up they had plenty of imitators, such as the Ken- tucky Minstrels, the Ethiopian Serenaders, the Congo Melodists and the African Minstrels. The best known minstrel group was Christy's Min- strels. They toured the South and West for four years. Then they performed in New York for seven years.

Christy's Minstrels and the other blackface groups claimed that they were performing authentic music of the southern slaves. Many of them did travel to the south and study with African American musicians on the plantations. And many of the minstrel songs were adapted in turn by the slaves. This process continued until it is sometimes impossible to tell whether a song began with the blackface singers or with the African Americans they imitated.

Steamboats such as the Natchez on the Mississippi replaced other types of riverboats because they could go upriver as well as down. Steamboats could also carry much more cargo, and passengers as well. They were dangerous, however. Coal or wood fires heated the water to produce the steam that powered the engines to turn the wheels. The boilers sometimes exploded under too much pressure, resulting in the loss of hundreds of lives.

Professional Song Writer

The song that got the attention of the entire nation was "Oh, Susanna."

Its sheet music sold more than 100,000 copies in an era when 5,000 sales was considered outstanding. Soon people all over the country were singing the same song. The gold prospectors who swarmed to California in 1849 adopted it as their unofficial anthem. And it crossed the oceans, becoming a hit in Europe and even as far away as India.

In the music and entertainment world today, songwriters who create popular songs such as "Oh! Susanna" become millionaires. Each time a compact disc or tape containing the song is sold, the writer gets a royalty payment. Each time the song is played on the radio, the writer gets paid. Each time a singer performs the song, the writer gets paid. If the song is used on a movie soundtrack, the writer is paid. Copyright laws protect songwriters and insure that their songs continue to be their property.

But the only copyrights at that time were the royalties on sheet music, the published form of music. The songwriter received a few cents, depending on his agreement with the publisher, for each

copy of the song that was sold. That was all. Once a performer had a copy of the song, it could be sung and played many times without making any money for its composer.

And Stephen didn't even get sheet music royalties. Morrison said that he gave the rights free to a Cincinnati publisher. He was also careless in handing out copies of his songs to minstrel groups and individual performers. Between 1848 and 1850 sixteen different music publishers brought out versions of "Oh! Susanna," and Stephen made no money on any of them.

Also, Stephen may not have been eager to claim that he had written a blackface song. His more romantic parlor ballads all had his name on them when they were published.

Even though he hadn't made much money so far, Stephen decided to make his living with his music. In 1849, he began his association with Firth, Pond & Co, a music publisher in New York City. They became the most successful in the country, largely because of Stephen Foster's songs.

One of the first songs Stephen sent to Firth, Pond was "Nellie Was a Lady," a minstrel song. It was unusual because it referred to Nellie, an African American, as a "lady." Previously the term had been applied only to white women.

In a very few years, with "Oh! Susanna," "Uncle Ned," and "Nellie Was a Lady," Foster had become a famous songwriter. He had another publisher, F.D. Benteen, in Baltimore. Fame, however, is not the same as money, and he had yet to show that he could make a living.

By early 1850, Stephen had quit his bookkeeping job in Cincinnati and was back in Pittsburgh. His father and mother, who had been living in boarding houses, moved with Stephen and his

This statue honoring Stephen Foster in Schenley Park in Pittsburgh demonstrates the city's pride in her native son. He was famous for his music during his lifetime, but received very little money for his songs although they were played and sung throughout the world.

brother Henry's family into a brick house owned by Brother William. It wasn't long before still another person joined the household.

When Stephen returned to Pittsburgh, he began seeing an attractive young woman named Jane McDowell. Jane already had a suitor, an attorney who was both wealthy and handsome. Descriptions of Stephen report that he was rather short—about five feet, seven inches—and thin, with dark eyes and straight dark hair. His shoulders drooped, and he habitually walked with his eyes lowered. This hardly sounds as though he was handsome, and he certainly wasn't wealthy. But he was determined.

His granddaughter tells the story of his proposal to Jane.

Both men called on Jane McDowell on the same evening. Stephen ignored the other caller, turned his back, and read a book. When calling hours were over at 10:30, the lawyer left. Jane came back into the room from showing her other suitor to the door and found Stephen facing her.

He said, "And now, Miss Jane, I want your answer. Is it yes, or is it no?"

The granddaughter continues, "Grandma, nineteen in years, unused to quick decisions, made one then." The decision was "yes."

They were married on July 22, 1850. Stephen mixed business with his honeymoon, traveling to the East Coast to meet both of his publishers. When they returned, they moved in with Stephen's family.

He was business-like about his songwriting. His studio was a third floor back room in the house. He had a chair and a piano, a music rack, a table and thick carpeting for soundproofing. In 1850 he published sixteen original works, and the same number in 1851.

But it wasn't easy. While many people believe that his songs poured out in flashes of inspiration, he actually worked very hard to make sure that the words and music were just right.

During the first few months of 1850, most of his published pieces were minstrel songs—probably some of them were written before he left Cincinnati. They were very popular, and his publishers wanted more. The best known of them was originally titled "Gwine to Run All Night," the song we now know as "Camptown Races."

After that, however, he didn't publish another blackface song for eight months. Instead he wrote the romantic parlor ballads that were popular among middle class ladies in the middle of the 19th Century. Ladies bought most of the sheet music.

Early in the spring of 1851, his father had a stroke that left him bedridden. Stephen became even more devoted to his mother, and influenced by her. Two of his songs of this time have themes related to her. The first, "Mother, Thou'rt Faithful to Me" is addressed specifically to her. The other is called "Farewell! Old Cottage." It seems to be an expression of Eliza's continuing grief over the loss of their home, the White Cottage.

While Stephen was caught up in his songwriting and in the concerns of his parents, his own family was growing. His daughter Marion was born on April 18, 1851. With a wife and child to support, it was clear that he had to return to writing blackface songs. He was going broke on romantic ballads. His average in royalties on songs written in standard English was $31 a song. For songs in blackface dialect the average was $319.44. That meant that he made ten times as much on the minstrel songs.

One of his most famous songs, "Old Folks at Home," was written at this time. Better known as "Swanee River," the song sold

even more copies than "Oh! Susanna" and became the best-selling piece of music ever written to that point. Some people even believe that it created the tourist industry in Florida, where the Suwannee River is located. And it became the official state song of Florida in 1935.

But Stephen sold the right to be listed as the song's author on the title page to George Christy of Christy's Minstrels. Not until the original copyright ran out over 25 years later did Stephen Foster's name appear on this, one of his most famous songs. He did, however, receive $1,600 in royalty payments. That was the most money he made for a song.

In February, 1852 Stephen and Jane Foster took a steamboat trip to the Mardi Gras in New Orleans on one of Dunning's boats. It was his first and only trip further south than Kentucky.

As they headed north a month later, people were rushing into bookstores to buy a new book. It was Harriet Beecher Stowe's novel, *Uncle Tom's Cabin*.

The book served as an inspiration to Foster. Soon he wrote one of his most famous songs, "My Old Kentucky Home, Goodnight," which was published the following January. It was originally called "Poor Uncle Tom, Good Night."

The new title eliminated the reference to Stowe's novel and blackface dialect. That way he freed his song from the politics of the time and allowed it to express timeless emotions of memory and loss.

When the song was published early in 1853, Stephen Foster was 27 and at the height of his fame.

Several weeks later, Jane Foster left her husband. ◆

HARRIET BEECHER STOWE

Harriet Beecher was born in Litchfield, Connecticut on June 14, 1811 into a religious, reform-minded family. Her father Lyman and brother Henry were both famous ministers. Her older sister Catharine founded a school for young women. Her younger sister Isabella was active in the movement to obtain the right for women to vote.

Harriet moved with her family to Cincinnati, Ohio in 1832. Two years later, when she was 23 years old, a collection of her short stories was published. In 1836, she married Calvin Stowe, a professor of Biblical Literature. During the first seven years of her marriage, Harriet had five children. She wrote magazine articles and short stories to help support the family.

Slave markets were active right across the Ohio River in Kentucky. Runaway slaves tried to cross the river to Ohio, which was a free state. The Beechers and the Stowes were abolitionists who tried to help the slaves escape. Harriet saw that the families of the slaves were broken up when they were sold to different owners.

In 1849, Harriet's little boy died of cholera. She experienced terrible grief at the loss of her child. It made her think of how much suffering that slave mothers endured when their children were taken away from them and sold.

In 1850, the Stowe family moved to Maine. At about the same time, the U.S. Congress passed the Fugitive Slave Act. Harriet thought that if she could write a story that would tell people of how the slaves suffered, then the laws could be changed. Her story was about a slave mother whose child was to be sold, so she ran away taking the child with her.

The editor of an anti-slavery magazine agreed to publish her story in 40 installments. The episodes became so popular that a Boston publisher wanted to publish them as a book. *Uncle Tom's Cabin* was published in March, 1852. It broke all sales records of the time, selling 3,000 copies the first day, 10,000 in a week, and 300,000 in the first year. The publisher had to keep his presses running day and night to keep up with the demand for the book. When Harriet Beecher Stowe met President Abraham Lincoln at a White House Reception during the Civil War, he said, "So this is the little lady who started this big war!"

This statue can be seen at "My Old Kentucky Home" State Park south of Louisville, Kentucky. It is on the grounds of Federal Hill Mansion, the home of the Rowan cousins whom Stephen Foster visited. Every summer at the park performers present "Stephen Foster- the Musical," featuring period costumes and more than 50 of his songs.

CHAPTER 5

Sad Songs

S tephen's drinking, which he began socially when he was one of the "Nice Young Men" in his early twenties, gradually had increased. And unlike his father, Stephen hadn't taken the temperance pledge.

Did Stephen's drinking cause the problems in his marriage, or did problems in the marriage cause him to drink more? Probably a combination of both. During the 19th Century alcoholism was not recognized as a disease. Alcoholics were considered sinners, and their families were ashamed of them. The Fosters were no exception.

There may have been another reason.

Jane wasn't really interested in Stephen's music and didn't understand why he needed to be alone when he was working on his songs. When she interrupted him, he would become very angry.

When Jane left, Stephen moved to New York City to be closer to music publishers. He enjoyed the city—maybe too much, because he did not write as many songs as he had in the previous years. Even though minstrel songs continued to be popular, Stephen Foster was no longer writing them.

He evidently missed Jane and Marion, because the songs he did write were about families. "Ellen Bayne" was about a beloved daughter. "Willie We Have Missed You" told the story of a husband's reunion with wife and children on Christmas Eve. "Jeanie with the Light Brown Hair" was written to his wife.

Some time early in 1854, Jane and Marion joined Stephen in New York. For a while the three of them lived in a boarding house. Years later Jane told her granddaughter that the landlady was so cheap and the food so scarce that there wasn't enough to eat. They left the place and moved across the Hudson River to a brick rowhouse in Hoboken, New Jersey.

Stephen and Jane stayed together in Hoboken less than a year. Stephen returned to his mother's house in Allegheny City in October. Times were hard in the Pittsburgh area. Unemployment was high and there had been a cholera epidemic. Stephen's response was one of his finest songs, "Hard Times Come Again No More." It has been revived many times by famous singers such as Bob Dylan, Nancy Griffith, Willie Nelson, and Emmylou Harris.

Stephen's mother Eliza died suddenly of a stroke early in 1855. Stephen took over the household and the care of his invalid father. Jane and Marion had rejoined him at this time. He wrote only four songs that year, but one of them, "Come Where My Love Lies Dreaming," was his most musically complex composition. This song was very popular with singers and orchestras because of its classical structure.

In July Stephen's father died. Shortly afterward he wrote another song about the pain drinking had caused his family, "Comrades, Fill No Glass for Me."

The family deaths continued the following year. Stephen's brother Dunning died of tuberculosis, and Brother William's sec-

ond wife also died. So it's not surprising that the one song Stephen published, "Gentle Annie," is a song of mourning. It was so successful that Firth, Pond issued a songbook, the *Gentle Annie Melodist*, which contained a collection of Foster's romantic ballads and none of his blackface songs. The preface of the book introduced Foster as "the most popular song writer of the present day."

Another reason for Stephen's lack of new songs was his involvement in politics. Although he had little interest in such things, his brother Morrison convinced him to participate. Morrison was a dedicated Democrat campaigning for James Buchanan in the 1856 presidential elections.

They formed the Allegheny Buchanan Glee Club with Stephen as the musical director. Much of his energy went into arranging music for this group, marching with them to campaign rallies and getting into hassles with Republican glee clubs. It was a great irritation that the Republicans used many of his tunes, such as "Nelly Bly" and "Camptown Races," for their campaign songs.

Buchanan won the election. But since he was not writing new songs, Stephen's financial situation became more and more desperate. Early in 1857, he sold the copyrights for all his songs to Firth, Pond for $1,872.28. Today, those rights would be worth millions.

For the next three years, Stephen, Jane and Marion lived in a series of dreary boarding houses. In the spring of 1860 they moved to Warren, Ohio to visit Stephen's sister Henrietta for several months. By autumn they were on their way to New York again.

Desperate for money, Foster wrote blackface songs. The greatest of these—and one of the most famous of all time—was "Old Black Joe." Written entirely without dialect, it confers dignity on an elderly slave in his final days.

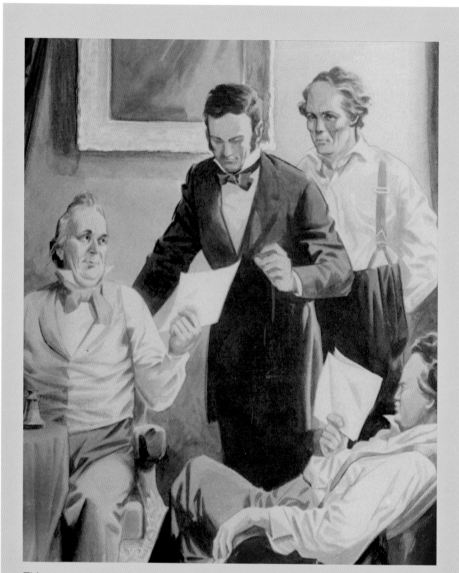

This watercolor painting shows President James Buchanan at work. Stephen Foster and his brother Morrison campaigned actively to elect Buchanan. Stephen was the musical director of the Allegheny Buchanan Glee Club. He arranged the music for this group, which marched at campaign rallies for Buchanan.

It was written during the great tumult that greeted the election of President Abraham Lincoln. Soon after, in 1861, the Civil War began. But Stephen Foster was too deeply sunk in his own troubles to pay much attention. "Old Black Joe" contained the lines "I'm coming. I'm coming. My head is bended low. I hear those gentle voices calling..." These lines may have reflected how tired he was becoming.

His wife Jane was also tired—tired of his drinking and tired of moving from one cheap boarding house to another. So she took their daughter and left for the last time. She became a telegraph operator to support herself and her daughter.

In New York Stephen continued to turn out song after song, no longer in hopes of earning much money. Now he only wanted money to buy rum. Although he was opposed to the war, he wrote a number of war songs. But none achieved the popularity of his earlier hits.

When Morrison sent him clothes so he wouldn't look shabby, he sold them for drinking money. Stephen's granddaughter recorded that when his brother complained of Stephen's appearance, he replied, "Don't worry about me. No gentleman will insult me, and no other can."

During his last year in New York, Stephen did much of his work in what was called a Grocery Liquor. These places were regular grocery stores with back rooms that sold cheap rum from a keg.

A law student and poet named George Cooper found Stephen there in the winter of 1862. Cooper had one of his poems with him and wanted it set to music. The composer took a crumpled sheet of music paper from his pocket, spread it out and began writing the music on an upturned cheese box. Then the two men set out through the slushy streets to sell their song.

That began a collaboration that produced more than twenty songs in the next year. Stephen called Cooper "the left wing of the song factory" because he wrote the words while Stephen composed the music. But there was still very little money coming in.

One day Stephen went to one of his publishers to ask for a few copies of one of his songs. He was turned down. A young woman in the office recognized him and asked, "Is this Mr. Foster?"

"Yes," he replied, "the wreck of Stephen Foster."

On January 10, 1864, Stephen woke up in the room of his Bowery hotel. But he had been weakened by a fever. He stumbled and fell against the wash stand, cutting a large gash in his neck. George Cooper was sent for and a doctor soon arrived. The two of them managed to get Stephen to Bellevue Hospital. Cooper wrote to Stephen's brothers and Jane, but Stephen Foster died on the afternoon of January 13 before they could get to New York.

In his wallet was a scrap of paper on which was written, "Dear friends and gentle hearts." Perhaps he intended it to be the words of a song.

He also had 38 cents, one penny for each year of his life. ◆

EMANCIPATION
PROCLAMATION

When Abraham Lincoln was elected President of the United States in 1860, the Southern states believed that he would abolish slavery.

While Lincoln personally believed that slavery was an evil institution, he thought that his first duty as president was to preserve the union. He tried to calm the fears of slave owners on the southern plantations. He assured them that he would not free the slaves. They didn't believe him. In 1861 these states seceded from the Union, beginning the American Civil War. Northerners thought that the war would soon be over. They were wrong. The South fought bravely and their generals were better than the Union generals.

The Union generals and many people in the government continued to put pressure on Lincoln to free the slaves. They thought that if the slaves were free they would help the Union soldiers. Each time the generals asked him he said no. He wanted the South to surrender and rejoin the Union.

In July of 1862, Lincoln drafted a "Preliminary Proclamation" and presented it to his Cabinet. The reaction of the Cabinet secretaries was mixed. The Secretary of War, Edwin M. Stanton, realized that it was a military measure that would weaken the South by depriving them of labor. It would also bring more men into the Union Army. Other members of the Cabinet were afraid that they would lose the next election if Lincoln freed the slaves.

But Lincoln went ahead. On January 1, 1863, he issued the Emancipation Proclamation. The first paragraph said, "That on the 1st day of January, A.D. 1863, all persons held as slaves within any State or designated part of a State the people whereof shall then be in rebellion against the United States shall be then, thenceforward, and forever free." It went on to say that the government of the United States would recognize and maintain their freedom.

The Emancipation Proclamation did not free all of the slaves. It applied only to slaves within the states fighting against the Union, not to slaves in the border states that had remained in the Union. The freedom of all slaves was not achieved until passage of the 13th Amendment to the Constitution in December 1865.

Selected Works

From the beginning, Stephen Foster's songs have created controversy. His minstrel songs were first attacked for the dialect they were written in because it was considered unrefined. Now that use of language is considered racist. Words like "nigger" and "darkies" are no longer acceptable. His romantic ballads have been criticized for being sentimental or morbid—or both.

But for all the controversy, his songs have continued to be popular for over 150 years. They have become genuine American folk music.

Minstrel Songs in Blackface Dialect
"Oh! Susanna"
"De Camptown Races"
"Lou'siana Belle"
"Old Folks at Home"
"Uncle Ned"
"Nellie Was a Lady"

Romantic Ballads
"Old Dog Tray"
"Jeanie with the Light Brown Hair"
"Beautiful Dreamer"
"Come Where My Love Lies Dreaming"
"My Old Kentucky Home, Goodnight!"

Spirituals
"Old Black Joe"
"Hard Times Come Again No More"

Chronology

1826	born on July 4 in White Cottage on Allegheny River
1827	White Cottage is sold and Foster family forced to move
1829	19-year-old sister, Charlotte Foster, dies of fever in Louisville, Kentucky
1833	father takes temperance pledge
1840	lives with older half-brother William; begins study at Athens Academy
1841	plays first composition, "The Tioga Waltz," on his flute at the Athens Presbyterian Church; enrolls at Jefferson College but leaves after one week
1844	publishes first song, "Open the Lattice Love"
1846	hired as bookkeeper by brother Dunning and moves to Cincinnati
1847	"Oh, Susanna" performed at Andrews' Eagle Ice Cream Saloon in Pittsburgh
1849	publishes "Nellie was a Lady"; signs publishing contract with Firth, Pond & Co. of New York
1850	marries Jane McDowell
1851	birth of daughter Marion
1852	travels by steamboat to New Orleans with Jane
1853	parts from wife and moves to New York
1855	mother and father die at family home in Allegheny
1856	becomes musical director of the Buchanan Glee Club
1860	moves to Warren, Ohio with Jane and Marion to live with sister Henrietta
1861	wife Jane leaves for final time, moving to Pennsylvania and finding work
1864	dies on January 13 at New York's Bellevue Hospital of injuries from a fall

Timeline in History

1820	Missouri Compromise sets off slavery controversy as Missouri is admitted to the Union as a slave state and Maine as a free state; slavery prohibited in portions of Louisiana Purchase north of Missouri's southern border
1825	Erie Canal opens
1826	Thomas Jefferson and John Adams, former U.S. presidents who signed the Declaration of Independence, both die on July 4
1831	Nat Turner leads slave rebellion in Virginia
1843	first blackface group, the Virginia Minstrels, is formed
1846	United States declares war on Mexico
1847	Frederick Douglass and Martin Delaney publish African American abolitionist newspaper the *North Star*
1848	Gold discovered at Sutter's Mill in California, beginning westward migration
1852	Harriet Beecher Stowe publishes *Uncle Tom's Cabin*
1859	John Brown and abolitionists attack federal arsenal at Harper's Ferry, Virginia
1860	Abraham Lincoln elected President
1861	Southern states secede from the Union to begin the Civil War
1863	President Abraham Lincoln issues Emancipation Proclamation freeing the Southern slaves
1865	13th Amendment to the U.S. Constitution outlaws slavery; Lee surrenders to Grant at Appomattox ending the Civil War; President Lincoln assassinated

For Further Reading

For Young Adults

McKissack, Patricia. *Frederick Douglass: Leader Against Slavery.* New Jersey: Enslow
    Publishers, 1991.
Purdy, Claire Lee. *He Heard America Sing: The Story of Stephen Foster.* New York: Julian
    Messner, Inc., 1940.
Sawyer, Kem Knapp. *The Underground Railroad in American History.* New Jersey:
    Enslow Publishers, 1997.

Works Consulted

Austin, William W. *Susanna, Jeanie, and the Old Folks at Home: The Songs of Stephen C.
    Foster From His Time to Ours,* Urbana and Chicago: University of Illinois Press,
    1987.
Bean, Annemarie, ed. *Inside the Minstrel Mask: Readings in Nineteenth Century Blackface
    Minstrelry, Wesleyan University Press, 1996.*
Emerson, Ken. *Doo-Dah! Stephen Foster and the Rise of American Popular Culture.* New
    York: Da Capo Press, 1998.
Howard, John Tasker. *Stephen Foster: America's Troubadour.* New York: Thomas Y.
    Crowell Company, 1953.
Morneweck, Evelyn Foster. *Chronicles of Stephen Foster's Family.* Pittsburgh: University
    of Pittsburgh Press, 1944.

On the Internet

Selected Poetry of Stephen C. Foster
http://www.library.utoronto.ca/utel/rp/authors/fosters.html

Stephen Collins Foster: America's Famous Folksong Writer, A Pictorial History
http://www.bobjanuary.com/foster/sfhome.htm

Stephen Collins Foster: Biographical Sketch
http://www.pitt.edu/-amerimus/foster.htm

American Experience: Stephen Foster
http://www.pbs.org/wgbh/amex/foster

Glossary

abolitionist (ab-oh-LISH-un-ist) – person who believes slavery should be abolished

alcoholic (al-co-HAWL-ik) – person addicted to alcohol

blackface (BLAK-face) – white minstrel comedian with burnt cork rubbed on his face to imitate an African American

boarding house (BORD-ing-hows) – house where people pay to live and have their meals

bounty (BOWN-tee) – sum of money given as a reward

cholera (CALL-er-uh) – disease of gastro-intestinal system often acquired by drinking impure water

collaborate (co-LAB-er-ate) – to work together

default (de-FAWLT) – failure to pay a debt

dialect (DYE-uh-lekt) – form of language different than standard educated use

flageolet (flad-juh-LET) – old-fashioned flute

foreclose (for-CLOZE) – take away property for non-payment

merchandise (MER-chun-dice) – goods bought and sold

minstrel (MIN-strul) – member of a band of public entertainers

royalty (ROY-ul-tee) – percentage of the sales figure of a literary or musical property

temperance (TEM-per-uns) – never drinking alcohol

tenant (TEN-unt) – person who rents a house, apartment, or office

thespian (THESS-pee-un) – actor

Index